Dandelions

Stars in the Grass

by Mia Posada

CAROLRHODA BOOKS, INC./MINNEAPOLIS

Carolrhoda Books, Inc.
A division of Lerner Publishing Group
241 First Avenue North
Minneapolis, MN 55401 U.S.A.

Website address: www.lernerbooks.com

Library of Congress Cataloging-in-Publication

Posada, Mia.
Dandelions: stars in the grass / by Mia Posada.
p. cm.
Summary: Rhyming text presents the dandelion, not as a weed, but as a flower of great beauty. Includes information about the flower, a recipe, and science activities.
ISBN 1-57505-383-7 (lib. bdg. : alk. paper)
1. Common dandelion—Juvenile literature. [1. Dandelions.] I. Title.
QK495.C74P67 2000
583'.99—dc21 98-53000

Manufactured in the United States of America
2 3 4 5 6 7 - JR - 06 05 04 03 02 01

To Raul

I know that some people
call it a weed,

but to me the dandelion
is a noble
breed.

Bright yellow petals
adorn each one,

spreading out
like rays of the sun.

In spring, dandelions bloom
like gold stars in the grass,

growing taller and taller as the warm days pass.

Under sunny summer skies,

the flowers are visited by
bees and butterflies.

The flowers begin to change
one summer day.
Their bright yellow petals fold up
and
fall
away.

In place of petals emerge fluffy tufts of white.

They
form
a perfect
circle,
delicate
and light.

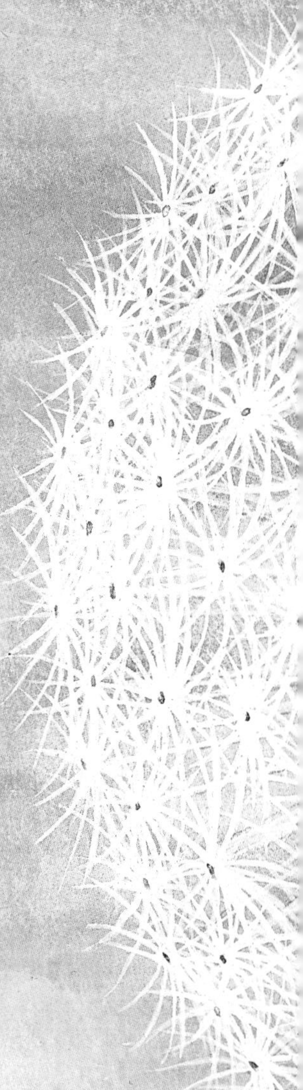

The wind blows them loose,

sweeping them into the sky.

Like tiny umbrellas

they float up high.

Every flying tuft the wind has freed
carries with it a tiny seed.

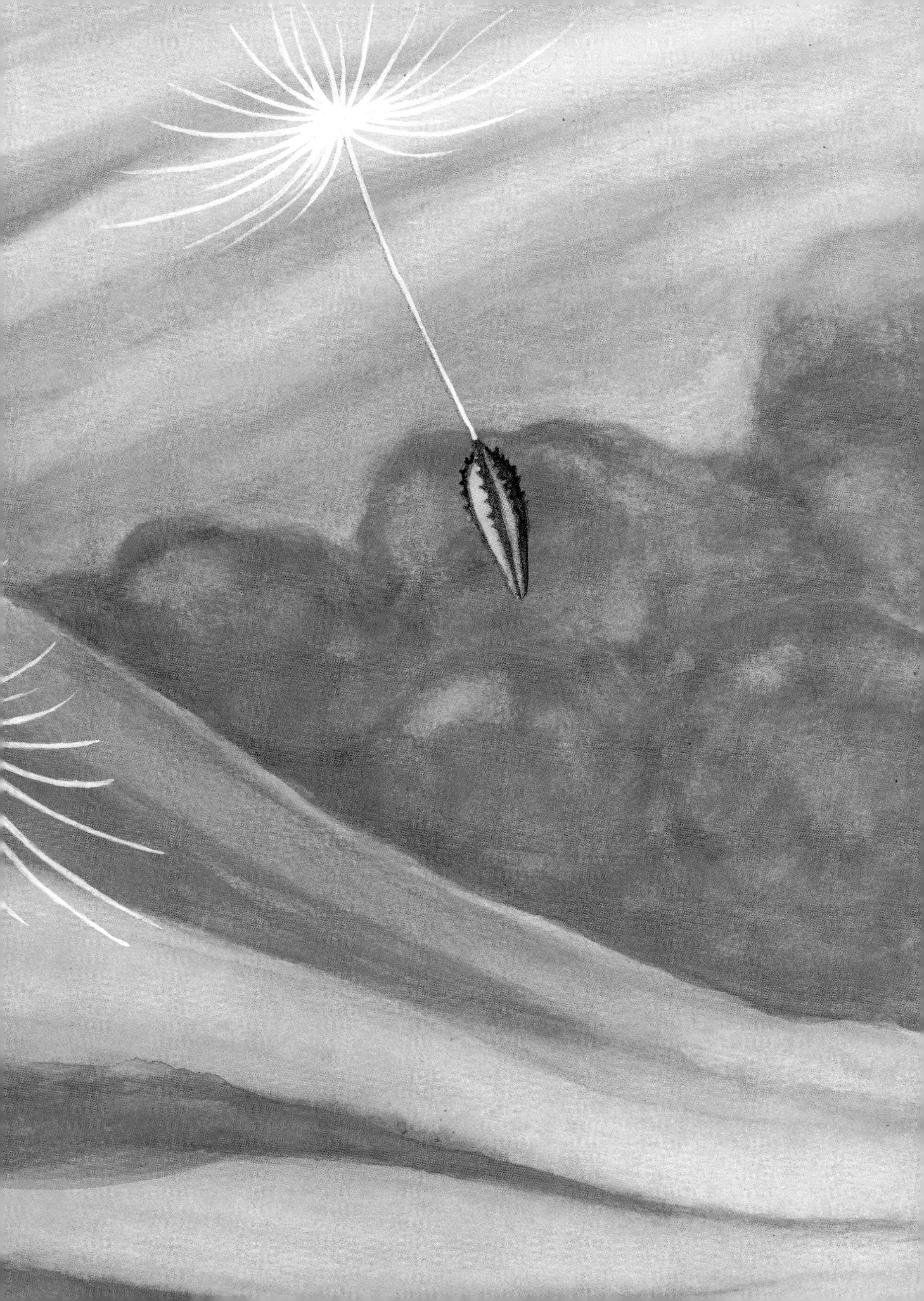

The tufts float on the wind
until falling to rest.
A nice grassy hillside
is what they like best.

Into the soil
a seed
snuggles
down.
Slender new
roots tunnel
deep underground.

Fragile green leaves begin to grow,

sprouting up

from the earth below.

Look closely and you'll find
round buds of green.
But bright yellow petals
are yet to be seen.

The buds slowly open, facing the sky.
Sunlight and water will help them grow high.

As summer moves on,
sunny and warm, seeds become flowers.

New dandelions form!

More about Dandelions

The name dandelion comes from the French *dent de lion*, or "lion's tooth." The scientific name for the dandelion is *Taraxacum officinale.* Dandelions belong to the same family as daisies and sunflowers. They are native to Europe and Asia but grow in temperate, or mild, climates around the world.

Dandelions are perennial flowers, which means a new plant can grow from an old root each year. They are also composite flowers. Every flower is actually many small flowers close together.

You can eat dandelion leaves and roots, but be sure they have never been sprayed or fertilized. Pick the greens in the spring before the flowers bloom. (Older leaves taste bitter.) The leaves of young plants contain large amounts of vitamins A and C and are eaten in salads.

Dandelions are not good garden plants because other plants do not grow well around them. This is because dandelions are very good at using up the nutrients, or food, in the soil. They grow quickly and are not easy to stop. For this reason, many people call them weeds. Dandelions may not be welcomed by gardeners, but as wildflowers, they add much beauty to the world.

Eating Weeds

Here's a modern version of a salad brought to America by German settlers. It's called *Zigorriesalat,* or lion's teeth salad. Make it yourself and try one of America's tastiest weeds.

4 cups dandelion greens*
6 hard-boiled eggs, chilled, peeled, and sliced
1 cup prepared creamy dill or creamy Italian salad dressing
salt and pepper to taste

1. After picking your dandelion greens (see CAUTION below), sort the leaves, throwing out the harder outer leaves. Separate the tender inner leaves, tearing them into bite-sized pieces. Wash well in cold water at least three times to get rid of sand or grit. Drain well.
2. Place eggs in a bowl. Add prepared salad dressing. Stir to mix.
3. Place greens in a big salad bowl. Add dressing and egg mixture. Toss together. Add salt and pepper to taste.

Serves 4 to 6

*CAUTION: Use only dandelion greens from an area that has never been sprayed or fertilized. Also, pick your greens early in the spring, before the flowers have bloomed, or the taste will be bitter.

Dandelion Science

By closely watching, or observing, dandelions, you can learn more about how they grow:

- Find a dandelion in bloom. Carefully observe the dandelion flower on a sunny day, first thing in the morning, at noon when the sun is high overhead, in the afternoon, and after sunset. What direction does the dandelion flower face at different times of day? Compare its motion to the path of the sun in the sky. When is the flower open? When is it closed? What conclusions can you make about how daylight affects dandelions?
- Cut a dandelion stem close to the base. Then remove the flower head. Look carefully at the stem. Can you see all the way through? Dandelion stems are hollow but sturdy.
- Dig a dandelion from the ground, being careful to remove as much of the root as possible. (Most people won't mind if you dig up a dandelion, but be sure to ask first for permission.) Is it hard to remove the root? How long is the dandelion's root? The dandelion's long, strong root is called a taproot. Why do you think its taproot helps the dandelion thrive?

- Cut off a dandelion flower in full bloom. Remember that dandelions are composite flowers, so you are really looking at a bouquet of flowers. How big is your bouquet? Try counting each flower, pulling the dandelion apart, yellow petal by yellow petal. Don't be surprised if you find two hundred or more individual flowers, or florets.
- Late in the spring or summer, find a dandelion that has formed a white, fluffy ball. This is often called a blowball. Where did it get its name? Try blowing on the ball of white and see. How far do the seeds travel after they leave the dandelion head? How do the blowball's parachute-like seeds help dandelions spread their seeds?

To learn even more about dandelions, read *Dandelions* by Kathleen V. Kudlinski (Lerner Publications Company, 1999). It's filled with facts and photos about this noble weed.